Robots A2Z

Robots A₂Z

by
Thomas H. Metos

illustrated with photographs

Julian Messner (M) New York

Library of Congress Cataloging in Publication Data

Metos, Thomas H
    Robots A$_2$Z.

      Includes index.
      SUMMARY: Discusses robots, automatons, and other
mechanical devices, the earliest of which was developed
as part of an Egyptian water clock around 2000 B.C.
      1. Automata—Juvenile literature. 2. Robots,
Industrial—Juvenile literature. 3. Androids—
Juvenile literature. [1. Automata. 2. Robots]
I. Title.
TJ2211.M47   629.8'92   80-21004
ISBN 0-671-34027-1

To my family

Messner books by Thomas H. Metos

Robots A_2Z
Exploring With Metrics *(with Gary G. Bitter)*
Exploring With Pocket Calculators *(with Gary G. Bitter)*
Exploring With Solar Energy *(with Gary G. Bitter)*

Acknowledgments

Grateful acknowledgment is made to companies and industries whose cooperation made this book possible.

American Media representing Quasar Industries, W.D. Hawley of Cincinnati Milacron, Digi Tech Incorporated, Gallaher Research Incorporated, Ken Davis of General Development Company, Erik Lindholm of Lour Sales Group, The Micro Works, Robot Institute of America, and Terrapin Incorporated.

Special recognition is given to Gene Beley of Android Amusement Corporation and J.F. Engelberger of Unimation Incorporated whose cooperation and kindnesses were most appreciated.

Finally, without the aid of Justin and Madelyn K. Anderson this book could not have been completed.

Contents

1   What is a Robot?   11

2   Robots in History   15

3   Robots Today   37

4   Robots in Movies and Television   48

5   Robots in Space and War   52

6   Robots Around the House   58

7   Robots of the Future   74

    Index   78

1 What is a Robot?

Tired of taking out the trash or cleaning your room? Want a pet that never has to be fed or walked but is always ready to play? What you may need is a robot. There are a number of people in the United States who have built their own robots to perform a variety of tasks around the house.

You may have been in a shopping center lately and seen an entertainment robot—singing, dancing, answering questions and generally attracting attention to some store or sale.

There are large companies today whose business is making robots for industry. And a number of university and research laboratories around the world are working on robot devices that may change the way the world lives and works.

The word *robot* belongs to the twentieth century. It

comes from the Czech word "robota," meaning forced labor. In 1921 the word "robot" was first used in a play by Karel Capek, called *R.U.R.* (Rossum's Universal Robots). The play dealt with the creation of robots who were meant to free humans from the drudgery of work. However, the robots were given human emotions by their creator. As a result, the robots discovered the desire for freedom and proceeded to destroy their human masters. The final scene of the play shows two robots as the Adam and Eve of the Robot Age.

In 1926, Fritz Lang's movie *Metropolis* brought robots to the screen. The major character was a female robot named Maria who wanted to punish and then destroy humanity.

Both *R.U.R.* and *Metropolis* started a trend of using robot characters in films, plays, and science fiction books.

The word "robot" is widely used—and sometimes misused. People often use the words "robot," "automaton," "android," or "humanoid" interchangeably though they are not the same. Such movies as *Star Wars* or TV shows like "Battlestar Gallactica" encourage the confusion. Many of the robots are really androids or humanoids, as they not only have human form but often exhibit some very human failings. Some definitions, therefore, are in order:

Robot. Generally a mechanical apparatus doing work of a human being. A robot does not have to look human but is able to perform human actions and functions.

Automaton. A mechanical figure or contrivance constructed to act as if by its own motive power.

Humanoid. A machine or robot which has human characteristics in its physical appearance.

Android. An automaton or robot that is human in appearance and may, in fact, duplicate some actions and functions of the human body.

A device as simple as a room thermostat is a robot. The thermostat senses changes in the room temperature, interprets them and then reacts. These really are decisions of the device as to whether to turn the furnace on or off.

Isaac Asimov, in his 1950 science fiction book, *I, Robot,* set down "laws" for robots. Though fictional, these laws are accepted and referred to by almost anyone writing or talking about robots. Asimov's three laws of robotics are:

1. A robot may not injure a human being or through inaction allow a human being to come to harm.

2. A robot must obey orders given it by human beings, except where such orders would conflict with the First Law.

3.   A robot must protect its own existence as long as such protection does not conflict with the First or Second Law.

From the coining of the term "robot," to Asimov's Three Laws of Robotics, was only thirty years. But interest in robots goes back many centuries. There is a rich and varied literature about robot devices.

2 Robots in History

Robot devices are nearly as old as humanity. The very earliest were masks, dolls, toys, or figurines, and often religious in nature. Most of these were simple, articulated devices—they had moveable parts.

Aside from these very early articulated figurines, the first robotic devices were probably the Egyptian water clocks of some two thousand years B.C. These were not true robots. They were automata—mechanical figures or contrivances which acted as if under their own power. Water-powered figures that would strike bells to show the passage of time.

These automata became more complicated over the years. Around 200 B.C., Hero of Alexander designed and built complicated, elaborate, and amusing automata. He made a steam-powered merry-go-round and a hydraulically powered statue of Hercules slaying a dragon. Hero was truly an inventive genius, but he was also a practical

A drawing of Hero of Alexander's mobile theater. Note the lower part which shows the fluid container and hydraulic pipes to power the theater.

craftsman. He wrote several textbooks dealing with physical laws and the applications of science. His automata were built to demonstrate various physical laws to his pupils in the most interesting way.

Hero's best known and most elaborate automaton was a mobile theater. A platform holding a large figure of the god Bacchus was set in motion by water pressure. When a fire was lit, he poured wine onto a panther at his feet, and at the same time milk flowed from his staff. Flowers appeared around the base while figures danced about. When the dance was over, Bacchus and the figure of the goddess Nike turned, and the platform returned to its starting place.

Hero's writings, discoveries, and constructions inspired others to build even more complicated automata. One device was said to have presented a play in several scenes, including storms and shipwrecks.

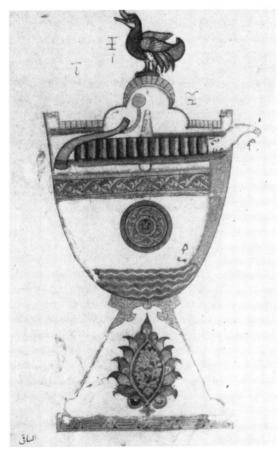

An early example of an automaton. When the cup was filled the bird would turn and whistle.

Though Hero's automata did not survive, his writings did. He was luckier than other inventors of automata, whose written evidence has been lost. One such person is Archytas of Tarentum, who, some 100 years before Hero, supposedly built a wooden pigeon that could take off, fly, and land like a real bird.

After Hero's time, there was little interest in automata until about 600 years ago, when the Chinese used a robot patient to train doctors in the use of acupuncture. Acupuncture is the practice of inserting needles into special points of the body to relieve pain and illness. The trainee inserted the acupuncture needles into the robot patient, a life-size bronze figure. If the needle was inserted correctly, the robot patient would squirt water out of the needle hole.

Complex automata appeared again in Europe at about the same time. One of the most fascinating is Albertus Magnus's automaton, a walking, talking servant. Magnus, a famous Bavarian philosopher, is supposed to have spent twenty to thirty years constructing it. There are several conflicting stories as to how the automaton worked, but they all indicate a remarkable device. One story refers to a mechanical figure which moved toward a door, answered it, and then saluted the visitor. In another version it was a figure of a beautiful woman who could talk.

Whatever the true version, they all end the same way. Saint Thomas Aquinas visited Magnus, saw the automaton and denounced it as a work of the Devil. He smashed it beyond repair—and with it twenty or more years of Magnus's work.

Others made impressive automata. Leonardo da Vinci made a mechanical walking lion. But most of the skilled makers of automata turned their talents to clocks.

If you live in a town with a large clock tower, or have seen one in a church or public building, the clock may operate with automata. Many of these are in the form of striking-jacks—figures, usually holding a hammer-like object, which strike the clock bells.

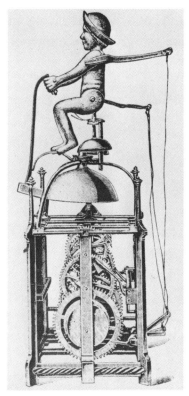

A striking-jack.

As time went on, the clocks—and their automata—became more complicated and intricate. The Strasbourg Cathedral clock has a great number of figures which move in various ways. A rooster crows and flaps its wings, fourteen angels with hammers strike the bells, a musician leads the angels and counts time, a figure of St. Peter goes through elaborate motions, figures of Vulcan and Hercules and several others move about. All of these figures are accompanied by bells and chimes. The clock at Strasbourg Cathedral is thought of as the greatest masterpiece of its kind. But other clocks were built in Europe, and later all over the world, all with automata.

As could be expected, people soon wanted clocks in their houses with automata like the great clock towers.

Several large striking-jacks on the front of an organ.

Most of those for the home were in the form of floor, table or mantlepiece clocks. Often intricately carved, sometimes jeweled, they had a variety of automata ranging from nativity scenes that moved, to revolving skeletons.

One household clock with automata that is still with us today is the cuckoo clock. It first appeared around 1730 and was the first of many clocks with singing or musical devices.

As interest in automata increased, many devices soon developed. They ranged from pocket watches, snuffboxes and walking-stick handles to mechanical pictures, picture clocks, and music boxes with moving figures of people or animals.

In the eighteenth and nineteenth centuries, a number of amazing and realistic automata were built. There were mechanical theaters, and creeping steel spiders, and one of the most exciting of automata, Vaucanson's mechanical duck, first exhibited in 1738.

Jacques de Vaucanson did not set out to invent a mechanical duck. His first interest was to create some kind of artificial life. But he ran out of money and decided to build a machine that would arouse public curiosity and raise money.

Vaucanson described his invention as "an artificial duck made of gilded copper, who drinks, eats, quacks, splashes about in the water, and digests his food like a living duck." Until recently, little was known about how the machine worked. The known pictures showed only

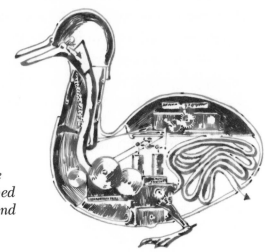

A drawing of Vaucanson's artificial duck, showing the internal works which allowed the duck to appear to eat and digest food.

the duck. Recently discovered pictures show the metal skeleton of the duck. It sat on a large box-like affair containing the mechanisms that powered the duck. An observer said:

> It is the most admirable thing imaginable, a piece of human workmanship almost passing understanding. Each feather of the wings is mobile and the anatomical structure of the duck is laid out in five parts . . . the artist walks up to the duck, which is placed on a pedestal . . . he touches a feather in the upper part of the bird, and we see the duck raise its head, look around in all directions, shake its tail, stretch itself, open its wings and flap them while

making a perfectly natural noise as if it were about to fly away. The effect is even more startling when the bird bends over its plate and begins to swallow grain with incredibly life-like movements. What will delight the expert is that the mechanism placed in the head and neck is in no way upset by all these movements and contortions and has no external support. No one has succeeded in explaining how the digestive process is achieved.

No one knows what happened to Vaucanson's duck or a similar mechanical duck built by Reichsteiner. They may have been destroyed—or maybe are still sitting in someone's attic in Europe. The secret of the duck, especially its digestive system, died with the two men. Reichsteiner said he had no desire to die without passing on his secrets, but he no longer had the mental ability to rebuild his marvelous mechanical duck.

Vaucanson was remarkable for more than his invention of the duck, for he was a skilled mechanical engineer—like many other creators of automata. His most important invention, the punched card that was to make possible the automatic loom for weaving cloth, was never used in his lifetime. Some years after his death, his invention was reconstructed and improved on by J.M. Jacquard. It was one of the most important inventions of the Industrial Revolution. Still later, the Jacquard card was to be the basis for today's computer punch card.

New types of automata started to appear. They were performing robots like the mechanical ducks, only most of them were in human form. These devices, called mechanical writers, were perhaps not as mystifying as mechanical ducks, but they were highly successful automata.

The first mechanical writers were made by Frederick Von Knaus. One of Von Knaus's machines had a small figure at the top of the mechanism. The figure wrote passages of varying lengths. The figure also dipped its pen into an inkwell to replenish the pen's ink supply.

Pierre Jaquet-Droz and his son were responsible for several mechanical writers. One of the main differences between their machines and Von Knaus's was the way they looked. Jaquet-Droz's first machines did not show the machinery, as Von Knaus's did, but only a very lifelike carved figure of a boy. "The figure, when writing, would start by dipping his pen in an inkwell, shake the pen twice, put his hand on top of the page and pause. Then the automaton is set to moving and the boy begins to write. He forms his letters carefully, distinguishing between light and heavy strokes."

Other people were soon building automatic writers. Many of them were constructed to draw instead of write. The pictures they drew ranged from simple outdoor scenes to intricately detailed ships.

These writing automata were only the beginning of a long line of performing robots, devices that danced,

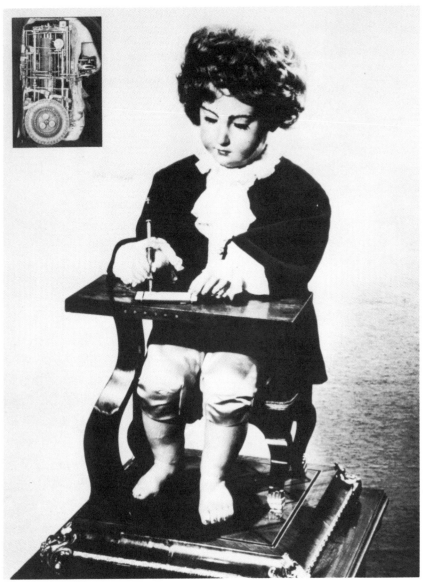

Jacquet-Droz's mechanical writer. The inset picture shows some of the mechanical workings of the writer.

A false hand that appeared to write. Used by a magician in his act.

walked, sang, and played musical instruments. There was even a woman who powdered her face.

A false automaton was probably the most famous of all performing robots. It was the "Chess Player" developed by Baron Wolfgang Von Kempelen, but best known as "Maelzel's Chess Player."

The story of the "Chess Player" is long and complicated. The idea of building it came from Baron Von Kempelen when he was summoned to the Austrian Court to give his opinion to the Empress on some magnetic games. Von Kempelen viewed the games and announced that he could build a much more lifelike machine which would be able to do surprising things.

In six months Von Kempelen presented his "Chess

Maelzel's Chess Player.

Player" to the world. It was immediately labeled "the most astonishing automaton that ever existed."

The "Chess Player" was a large box-like structure with a chessboard on top. Behind the box was the figure of a player.

Wherever Von Kempelen exhibited his creation, the inventor went to great lengths to assure the onlooker that no human being was hidden in the box to make the chess moves.

Von Kempelen took his machine across Europe. It was a most successful chess player—it even checkmated Napoleon I. Von Kempelen eventually sold his machine to a man called Anthon who exhibited it all over the world. Later it became the property of Leonard Maelzel, who worked at the Austrian Court.

Most people were convinced that Maelzel's "Chess Player" was truly an automaton capable of playing chess. But some were sure it was a fraud. One of these was the American author, Edgar Allan Poe. He remembered that at the exhibition he had attended, great care was taken to demonstrate that no human was hidden in the device. Yet Poe became certain that it was a fraud. He wrote a story proving through reason and logic that there had to be a person hidden in the "Chess Player." He was right.

Baron Von Kempelen's "Chess Player" did indeed turn out to be a fraud. But the Baron is credited with developing the first true automaton that could talk—it could reproduce human speech through the use of air pipes.

28

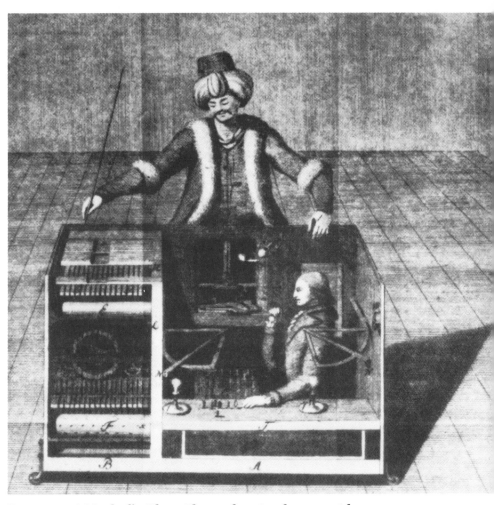

Drawing of Maelzel's Chess Player showing how a midget could be hidden inside.

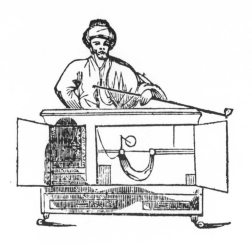

Edgar Allan Poe's conception of how a human being could be hidden in the Chess Player.

This so-called "talking head" became quite famous.

A true robot, made by J.N. Malkelyne in the 1870s, was Psycho, a dwarf figure who sat behind a small platform. Psycho could perform a variety of tasks: it could nod, shake hands, solve mathematical problems, smoke, and perform magical tricks. But its most famous accomplishment was playing cards—and winning. In several thousand card games, Psycho lost to human beings no more than a dozen times.

Thomas Edison, inventor of the electric bulb and phonograph, among other things, started producing talking children's dolls. A phonograph was inserted in

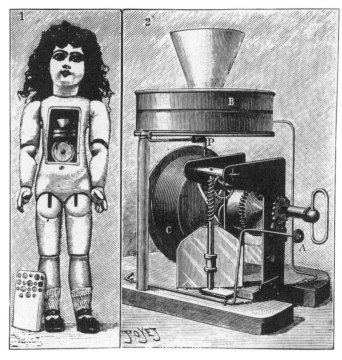

Edison's talking doll. On the right is the phonograph that was inserted into the body of the doll.

31

the doll, and when a crank on its back was turned, the doll recited a nursery rhyme.

Though automata and robot devices continued to be developed into the 1900s and beyond, industrial developments and inventions like the light bulb, phonograph, motion pictures and the automobile interested people more. However, at the 1939 World's Fair, in New York City, the robot Elektro and his dog

Automata that played cards, played music and drew pictures that were exhibited in 1876.

A toy knife-sharpening automaton.

Sparko were exhibited. They were shown as curiosities rather than as examples of technology. Elektro could count, smoke, recite, and his dog could beg, bark and wag his tail.

There is a story about a robot dog built for the World's Fair. Maybe it was Sparko—or there may have been another robot dog. No one knows. The dog had built-in sensing devices for heat and light. As the story goes, just

*A cigar lighting automaton. When a button was
pressed, the lighted arm would swing up.*

before the opening of the Fair, a passing car's headlights
attracted the robot dog. It dashed out and was crushed
by the wheels of the car.

In World War II, the technology of automata and
robotic devices was applied to the fighting of the war.

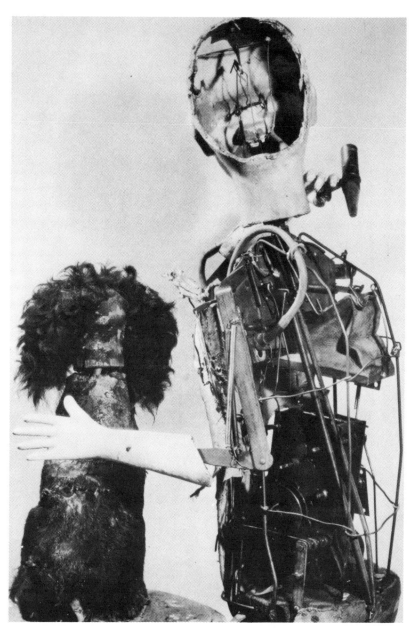

*The mechanical interior of an automaton that was used in the
early 20th century as part of a display in a department store.*

And ideas about robots started to change. Robots were thought of differently—not as Maelzel's Chess Player or as automata to entertain, but as devices to free human beings from labor.

3 Robots Today

Many of the early automata paved the way for today's robotic devices. From Hero's hydraulically powered creations to Vaucanson's invention of the punched card—so important to today's computers—those early devices were more than just entertaining. Because of their work, and the development of automatic machinery, functioning robots are here today.

There are many thousand robotic devices in industrial use worldwide, with more being added every day. Movies, television, and science fiction books are increasing interest in robots and their uses. Robots are already being used extensively in industry and in space exploration. The military in many countries are even investigating the use of robot soldiers.

Robots in Industry

A worker who never tires, works overtime without extra

pay, never goes on strike, never needs a lunch or coffee break, and never talks back to the boss: that's an industrial robot. The manufacture of industrial robots are one of the new growth industries in the world today. Industrial robots are different from automatic machines. Robots can change jobs, or change the way they do jobs. Automatic machines have to be junked or redesigned if their specific job is discontinued.

Since the 1950s, the use of computers in machines led to further development of industrial robots. We may soon have factories which are completely robot-operated, with only a human or two to make sure nothing goes wrong.

Why is the use of robots increasing? One answer is that a human worker can make mistakes, tires easily, needs time off, and is unable to handle certain dangerous situations.

But the most important reason for using robots is economic. Their work is reliable—done the same way all the time—and robot costs are lower than for human workers. In some industries the cost per hour for a robot worker is one-third less than for a human. And robots can work twenty-four hours a day, seven days a week, if need be.

Most industrial robots do not look like what you might think. They are often just a box with a mechanical arm and hand.

Industrial robots must meet at least three requirements. One, they must be capable of performing many different jobs. Two, they must be highly reliable. The breakdown of a robot causes the assembly line to stop, costing the industry time and money. And three, they must be easily taught to do their job.

Most robots used in factories have one arm, though robots are now being developed with two or more arms. The arm of the robot rests on a pedestal or large box which can turn so the arm has a more useful motion. The robot's arm has the roughly the same kinds of motions as

An industrial robot showing the control unit and the various movements it can make.

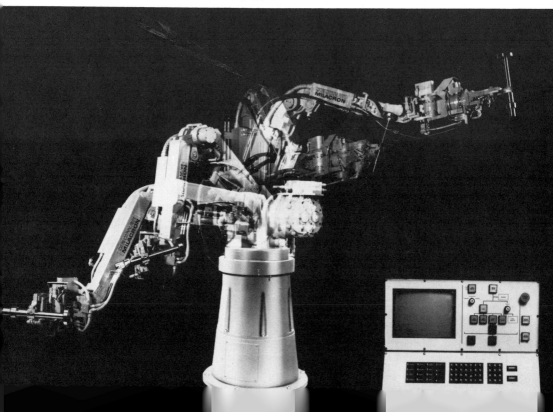

a human arm. There is a shoulder which moves up and down, an elbow which moves, and a wrist which can bend or swivel. Some robot arms can also extend and retract through the use of built-in extenders.

Industrial robots are mostly powered by electricity. Pneumatic or air pressure is also used. And to do heavy work, a robot powered by hydraulic or fluid pressure is needed.

Most robots used in industry are programmed. A human operator shows the robot what to do, and it remembers to do the task over and over again the same way it was taught. Programming can be done by using a simple control device that looks like a hand calculator. Other robots are controlled by programming a small computer that allows the robot to make decisions. A computer-controlled robot has sensors which feed back information reporting how the work is being done. If something goes wrong, the computer can have the robot approach its work in a different way. A computer-controlled robot can even tell by itself if something needs to be fixed.

Robots are presently used to spray paint, load and unload materials, weld, handle hot materials in forging plants, inject plastic into molds, cast, place and remove materials in other machines, and do many other jobs.

There are small portable robots that one company calls "apprentice robots." These are light robots which can be moved easily from place to place to do a job. One use of

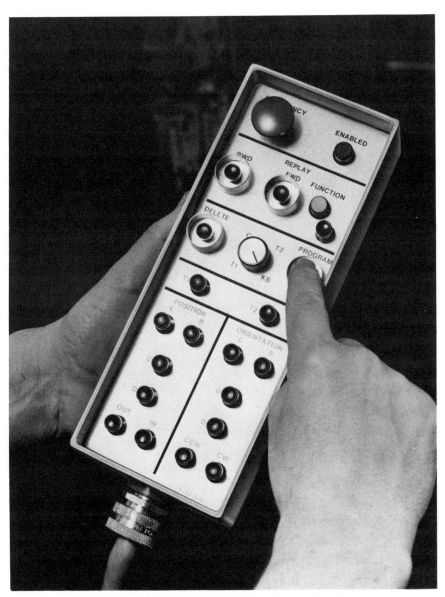

The control and "teaching" unit for an industrial robot.

41

The industrial robot is extracting a hot part from a die casting and dunking it into a quench tank, a hot and dangerous job.

these apprentice robots is in welding the bottoms of ships, a dangerous and unpleasant job for human beings.

Robots are being used to handle hazardous materials,

or to work where there are dangerous fumes, in mines, nuclear power plants, foundries and steel mills, under the ocean, and in space. There are even traffic robots to control traffic on heavily traveled streets when the roads are being repaired or built.

A robot welder.

An industrial robot that is used to make wax molds.

When an accident occurred in 1979 in the Three Mile Island Nuclear Power Plant in Pennsylvania, "Herman the Robot" was sent from the U.S. Department of Energy. "Herman" could go into the highly radioactive areas of the plant which no human being could enter.

Herman is mounted on tracks with TV cameras, and can be controlled from outside the plant by a 700-foot

Another hot and dangerous job. The robot is loading harrow discs onto the hearth of a heating furnace.

cable. Around six feet tall and five feet wide, Herman can lift 160 pounds, and drag 500 pounds. With its arm and hand, and with views from the two TV cameras for guidance, Herman helped turn off valves and do other necessary tasks in highly dangerous radioactive places in the plant.

Robots in the Office

Robots are already in use in the office as well as the factory. These robots are usually less complex and can therefore do less.

The most common example of the office robot is the Mailmobile, widely used in Federal offices in Washington, D.C. The Mailmobile looks even less like a robot than most. It is a five-foot cart with numerous open slots for the mail. The robot is powered by electric batteries and follows invisible chemical tracks painted on the floor. It stops at designated places for twenty seconds or so to deliver or pick up mail. As it goes from office to office, the Mailmobile announces its coming with a beeping noise. It is also equipped with a device to keep it from running over people.

The Mailmobiles don't miss as much as work as people —only about two hours a year for repairs.

Human employees have generally accepted the robot mail carriers, often giving them nicknames. In one office the robot is equipped with a radio and tape deck and goes around the building singing "You are the Sunshine of My Life." At Christmas the tune is changed to "Jingle Bells."

Mailmobiles, traffic robots, and some of the other robots doing simple, repetitive jobs, are lower order robots. They can only do a simple job in one way. Sometimes, they can also respond to a certain, simple, input.

Even the more complicated computerized industrial robots which can make decisions are, compared to humans, quite elementary. They can learn, act, and react to the environment or work conditions in only a few ways. But technological improvements in these robots are being made daily.

One company is now building industrial robots that can "see" and "feel." Through the use of cameras, these robots can tell the difference between a faulty and a perfect product. Also, through the use of sensors, they can detect the presence of objects, and know if they are in the right place or not.

These robots often play cards or dice in demonstrations to show how efficient their sensors are.

Yet even robots that can "see" and "feel" will not completely replace human workers in the foreseeable future.

4 Robots in Movies and Television

Star Wars, Battlestar Gallactica, The Black Hole, Lost in Space, Sleeper, War of the Worlds, Tobar the Great, Forbidden Planet, The Phantom Empire, Star Trek, The Day The Earth Stood Still, and *The Empire Strikes Back* are all movies or TV shows starring such amazing characters as Robby, R2D2, C3PO, Ceylon, Maria, Gort, V.I.N.CENT, and Maximilian—all robots. And this is only a partial list.

There has been an almost unending stream of plays, movies, stories, and more recently, television shows about robots. In all of these, the authors have appealed to our curiosity about mechanical beings as well as to our fear of a future controlled by machine beings.

Sometimes the robot is the "good guy," sometimes the "bad guy." Often they are clumsy creations but sometimes they seem so real that they make us afraid. The only trouble with all these robots is that the technology Hollywood has given them is not real. Most are simply actors *dressed* in costumes.

Probably the most popular of recent robot creations have been those in the movie *Star Wars*. The robots CP3O and R2D2 captured almost everyone's imagination. The high-polished C3PO with its almost human form seemed to be the ultimate android. It could walk, talk, and think, and its emotions were human. R2D2 was not humanoid in form and could not talk, but the squeaky noises coming from it did make R2D2 seem almost human.

Building and designing these two robots was very complicated. C3PO did not cause major problems because of its size and humanoid form. The problem with R2D2 was much greater. The most immediate one was to find a human being small enough to fit inside the robot shell. Yet the person had to have the strength and coordination to operate it. R2D2 also had to be designed for walking, and the human operator had to be able to see and to move the robot's arms. The operator also had to be able to do the fine motions necessary to grasp objects.

As if these problems were not enough, a second model of R2D2 was built to be radio-operated and steerable. To make the robot steerable at higher speeds, a third leg was added, which allowed the robot to turn. The robots were powered with six-volt jelly batteries operating a variety of mechanisms. The final results were extremely realistic and successful.

Robbie, Gronk, and even the computer HAL in *2001* have also stirred our imagination. But other movie and television robots have often been clumsy and sometimes the human operator has even been visible inside the robot skin.

Perhaps the most realistic robots are the creations in Disneyland and Disneyworld. Most of them represent human beings and animals. These robots are controlled through a system that Disney called *audio-animatronics:* a blending of animated techniques, computer, and sound. This system allows a technician to sit at a computer console and monitor, record, edit, and erase the commands to the robot. And, at the same time, the technician can blend the necessary sound track and lighting to the robot's movements. The use of the space-age technology of audio-animatronics and the Disney studio's creative skills have combined to produce many exciting exhibits for these entertainment parks.

The first of Disney's robots was the Enchanted Tiki Room, a tropical setting of palm trees, flowers, plants, and birds. Set into motion by the electric impulses of the computer, the audio-animatronic system causes the birds to sing, talk, and move. There is even a jungle storm.

An even more impressive robot show is the General Electric Carousel of Progress. This is rather like a play in a theater, only the theater revolves instead of the stage.

Each act of the play shows the impact of technology on the American family from the 1890s to the present, and then projects the family of the future.

Our main interest, though, is not the play but the players. The scenes are played by humanoid robots, with a robot dog for good measure. The robots are powered by air and fluid, which makes them very flexible and gives them a remarkably lifelike appearance. Along with their lifelike action, a complex sound system makes one feel as if the robots were actually speaking. In the end one even wonders if they are real or not. . . .

One Disney creation that has caused a great deal of comment is the robot figure of Abraham Lincoln. Many who have seen the robot President felt that they were seeing Lincoln brought to life again. This feeling was created by the sixty-five different movements the robot is capable of making. It has seventeen different expressions. The eyes move from side to side as if looking over the audience, and even the eyelids flutter.

Robot creations of the Disney Corporation may be the first of an improved generation of robots capable of operating without any support or direct controls.

5 Robots in Space and War

The exploration of space is of great—and growing—interest. Unfortunately, movies and television have given us the idea that space exploration is easy. But outer space is extremely hostile and dangerous—lack of air, extreme temperatures, and other dangers restrict us as space explorers. Using robots has helped us to explore without risking human life.

Robots are well suited for work in space. They do not require heavy and bulky life-support systems. They can work on a planet where human beings cannot. They don't need company to keep from getting lonely. They can even repair themselves, if need be, on radio command from Earth. The robot can be, and has been, a dependable, capable and reliable space explorer.

Robots have been to the moon and Mars. The Viking landers are the most complex space robots so far constructed. The Vikings are not humanoid in shape. They look more like a giant, metallic bug, complete with television antenna.

The Viking landers did a number of different jobs. They collected soil samples, detected planet quakes and tremors with a seismometer, measured the force and direction of the wind and took pictures. They analyzed soil and air samples, measured X-rays, and reported on

The Viking Lander is a robot.

weather conditions. They even carried a biological and chemical processor to conduct experiments and detect life.

We will be seeing even more robots in space in the years ahead. Space Shuttle flights will make great use of robots for monitoring, serving as backup units, and helping to maintain the control and power units.

One robot that doesn't make the headlines like the space exploring robots is one that has been around since 1929. In 1929 it was called the Link Trainer. Today this robot device is called a flight simulator.

The Link Trainer was used extensively during World War II to train pilots for wartime flying. What the Trainer did was to recreate, as closely as possible, the cockpit, controls, and conditions a pilot would face when flying a real airplane. The Trainer, which looked like a stunted airplane, dipped and banked when the trainee adjusted the controls. The Link Trainer enabled the armed forces to train more pilots faster, and more safely.

Today's robot descendant of the Link Trainer are the flight simulators. Very much more sophisticated, they range in price from $4,600,000 to $13,000,000. These flight simulators are a far cry from the old Link Trainers. They do the same job, but in a more realistic way.

The simulator looks like a space vehicle. It is box-like with long metal legs. Once you are in the pilot's seat and start the engines, which you hear and feel, the airport runway seems to stretch ahead. Taxi and takeoff instructions come over the radio. As you move the throttles, you feel the plane increase speed. The engine noise grows louder and louder. Down the runway you go, gaining speed, and when the wheel is pulled back you can feel the plane "take off" and then the thump of the landing gear as you retract it. And, as the plane moves away from the airport, you see the lights of Los Angeles below, and soon the screen shows the Pacific Ocean. You forget you are not flying a real plane.

The flight simulators save the cost of real planes, fuel, and, most importantly, lives. Training accidents, some fatal, occur every year with real planes. Simulators also give training in conditions one would never try for on a training flight, since the chances of accident would be too great.

The pilots who receive training in flight simulators are not beginners. They usually have thousands of hours of flight time. They are being trained to fly different models and types of planes from the ones they know.

Pilots are trained on simulators for commercial airlines, but the military in many countries are also using simulators to train fighter and bomber pilots. Military pilots in simulators are often trained in combat conditions and if an error is made, they are "shot down." For the military, the advantages of using flight simulators are the same as for commercial airlines: lives, time, money, fuel, and materials.

The military is also using a variety of robot weapons,

such as robot bombs and missiles, observation satellites, and attack satellites. But the age of robot soldiers has not yet arrived. However, much thinking and research is going on in various countries around the world into the development of robot soldiers.

Robot soldiers would be very advantageous. The major advantage, of course, would be the ability to fight battles without risking human life. The supply and support services for robot soldiers would also be much simpler than for human soldiers. They would not need food, shelter, or medical facilities as we know them today.

Robot soldiers would also be vastly superior to human soldiers if nuclear weapons were used. They would not be able to withstand direct nuclear explosions, but would be able to operate in highly radioactive areas without harm. Robots would also be safe from nerve gas and other chemical weapons. Maybe robots would end wars.

Once robot soldiers are developed, a very possible spin-off would be crime-fighter robots: security or guard robots for civilian life. They would carry, or have built in, a variety of weapons that need not kill, but would make a criminal helpless for a short period of time. Some weapons might be ultrasonic sound waves which would temporarily paralyze, laser or light rays which would temporarily blind, or sprays of tear gas or laughing gas. Or the weapon might simply be the use of superior strength or speed of the robot.

Security robots could have an even more amazing array of weapons: their sensor systems. Using its built-in electronic sensors, a security robot could easily detect the breathing, whispers, and even the heartbeats of intruders. Other sensors could detect the body heat, movement, or the vibration caused by muffled footsteps. Some security robots would have metal detectors, too. If someone tried to smuggle a gun past the robot, it would immediately move to block the passage. As you see, security robots or robot soldiers could be formidable opponents. And even more frightening in the wrong hands.

These soldier, security, and guard robots may be here sooner than we think. A great deal of work along these lines is being carried on by the military and certain civilian companies. Robot tanks are already being built, and security agencies do have the sensor technology available to build highly maneuverable robots with an intelligent consciousness—certainly not as great as humans, but at least intelligent enough to be able to make certain decisions. These kinds of robots must have an artificial intelligence that allows them to know when to kill, paralyze, or capture an opponent, be it human or robot. This intelligence, along with "hearing" and "seeing" sensors, would allow them to move in directions preplanned by human controllers, or to make tactical decisions on their own, such as whether to advance or retreat.

6 Robots Around the House

By now you probably think that robots are very expensive and only for use in industry and the military. This is not necessarily true. There are hundreds of people in the United States who have built, or are now building, their own robots: robot pets, household robots, or entertainment robots. Some are made by individuals themselves from scratch, others from kits available from several different manufacturers.

Therefore, it is not impossible for you to build your own robot. But it can be time-consuming and more than you probably can afford. If you do decide that you want your own "personal" robot, you may want to look at the toy robot market. Today there are a variety of toy robots for sale, ranging from ones that do nothing, to those that are highly sophisticated and perform amazing tricks or tasks.

Many of the robot toys that have appeared recently

AROK, built by Ben Skora, is one of the first home and entertainment robots.

are electrically powered and usually perform their feats using electronic chips, miniature parts, in much the same way as a pocket calculator. Some of the toys are android in form, while others are box-like with push buttons to activate them, the way you use a calculator. Some of these robots can even speak or spell.

Many of these robot toys are meant to entertain, just like the ancient automata. With their flashing lights, beeping noises, or their synthetic voices, they play games like chess and cards. Some will teach you how to spell or multiply, others can be programmed just to have fun watching them travel around the house and yard dodging all the obstacles, or picking up things. Several robots are modeled after such popular movie robots as R2D2 or

C3PO. One is patterned after a futuristic android robot and can breathe heavily, flash its eyes, and make assorted noises as if from outer space.

Many of these robot toys are expensive. One that sells for over $2,000 plays an extraordinary game about invading space aliens.

However, if you are handy with a soldering iron and can follow directions, kits are available from electronic stores and suppliers at much less cost. These electronic robot toy kits are also often greatly superior to ready-made ones.

Robots built by individuals are much more exciting than toy robots, because they can do so much more than toys. Several of the kit robots can be hooked up to a home computer or micro-processor which increases the number of things the robot can do.

Pet robots, for the most part, are less than satisfactory. You can't really pet one. They come in a variety of shapes and sizes and some can be made from kits. One was recently built by a sixteen-year-old high school student. This pet robot is called Mike. He doesn't look like an animal. He is a steel framework box on wheels. Mike has a small computer for a brain and understands spoken commands such as "go," "stop," "fast," and "back wards." He can roll around a room with ease. Mike is able to send out high-pitched sound waves, and from the echoes bouncing off the walls and chairs, knows to move out of the way. Even if he does hit something, Mike automatically backs up, turns around and heads in another direction.

In contrast to Mike, another pet robot called Buster just wandered aimlessly about until its batteries ran low. But then it immediately found an electrical outlet to recharge itself.

Probably the most popular robot pet is—the mouse. There is a very good reason for this: the Amazing Micro-Mouse Contest which draws over 6,000 entries. The object is to build a self-contained robot mouse that can find its way through a maze. Though most of the robots don't really look like mice, some have ears or a mouse-like body over electronic parts.

Getting to the finals of the Amazing Micro-Mouse Contest is quite difficult because of the number and high quality of the entrants. One person borrowed an experimental electronic part worth over a million dollars from his company to help his mouse go faster through the maze!

The robot mice are usually of two types. There is the mechanical type, called "wall huggers," which don't learn the maze but move quickly. The other type is usually electronic, fitted with a mini-computer and sensing devices to detect walls and turns. These devices enable the mouse to remember the mistakes it makes and so it learns to run the maze faster and with fewer errors.

Even with these electronic aids, the winner of the $1,000 prize in 1979 was a mechanical "wall hugger," called "The Moonlight Flash."

If you are serious about building or acquiring your own mechanical robot, you have to know what is involved. You have to be knowledgeable in electronics, mechanics, and mathematics. Many of the kits must be assembled—and are quite expensive. In fact, it is not uncommon for individuals who build their own robots to spend from ten to fifty thousand dollars! However, if you still would like to try, there are several books available either in your library or at technical bookstores that can help you understand the problems of building a robot.

A number of companies sell kits and fully assembled robots. Many of them must be hooked up to a small computer or micro-processor to function fully. Some of these robots are very limited in what they can do, while others are limited only by the time, money, and ingenuity of the builder.

The following represents a small part of the robot kits and fully assembled models available right now. And every day new kits and new robot companies are being formed.

One of the smallest and least expensive kits is the Turtle, by Terrapin, Inc., called that because it is about the size of a box turtle. The plastic dome, about seven inches across, sits on a chassis, and has two large wheels capable of moving six inches a second. As the wheels can

The completed Turtle.

turn in opposite directions, the Turtle can turn on the spot and move in any direction. It can also "talk" with its beeper, and flash its lights.

The plastic shell of the Turtle has a sensor built into it so that it can "feel" or "sense." When it bumps into objects it will stop and move in another direction. Also built into the body is a pen. When this is lowered, it allows the Turtle to draw. However, in order to do these and other things, the Turtle must be hooked up to a small computer. When properly connected and programmed, the Turtle can travel through mazes. And, when the information is stored in the computer's memory, it can draw a map of a room it has explored.

The Turtle can do other, even more complicated things, depending on the computer, the way the Turtle is programmed to react, and the imagination of the owner. If a scoop or hand is attached, it can push objects around and pick them up. It can even help students learn geometry.

Another robot kit on the market today is et-2, manufactured by Lour Control Group. This robot is advertised as "a robot that won't do a darn thing . . ." until you add your own electronic controls. Et-2 is about two feet high, three-wheeled, and shaped rather like a cart. Lour Control provides a shell, power drive, and gears in a complete package. Et-2 can be operated off its own battery and can therefore be independent of other power sources.

The company is planning to provide a manipulator, or hand, to be mounted on the front of the shell, an ultrasonic detector for range and object location, and a directional light-seeking sensor that will cause et-2 to drive toward any light source. If you had these additions, plus your own electronic controls, et-2 could be a remarkable home robot. It could be programmed to move around the house without bumping into furniture, grasp and pick up light objects, and even answer the door.

et-2 ready to be connected to a computer.

A third robot kit on the market is the Grivet series developed by John Gallaher. The Grivet is essentially a moveable hand and arm that can be used with a home computer or micro-processor. It can be mounted on a mobile electric cart, or on a number of different mounts, so that it can easily do various tasks. Grivet can even play

The Grivet making the first move in a chess game.

chess. It can even be fitted with an "eye" so that the computer it is attached to can "see" what it is doing. This eye is a video camera hooked up to a special part or chip in the computer. The use of the "eye" allows the Grivet to transmit pictures and to see and react to whatever task it has been assigned to do.

Though you may not have seen a home robot, you may have seen an entertainment robot attracting shoppers to a store or shopping center. Entertainment robots are a combination of home robots, industrial robots, and some are right off the motion picture screen. Entertainment robots are usually built by people who are very interested in robotics. They may have built their own robots and have gone on to build entertainment robots to be rented or sold.

There are a variety of entertainment robots being used around the country. Gene Beley of Android Amusement has built several different types. These range from a robot seven feet, nine inches tall, called Ralph Roger Robot, to a small robot called Six, which resembles R2D2 of *Star Wars*. Beley has recently built two show robots which are android in form. These androids, called Andrea and Adam, have been highly effective as entertainers and in attracting crowds. The androids ask people questions, and many people find themselves responding as if to a real human being. The androids are startlingly human in form, and can be dressed for any occasion, from formal to casual wear. Their faces can

Six, Ralph Roger Robot, Adam (in two parts), and Andrea Android ready to go to an exhibit.

John, Shawn, Michael, David, Lorie, Melisa, and Jason are meeting Andrea Android for the first time.

even be changed to those of male or female celebrities when desired. The robots can shake hands, dance, and move their heads.

Costing from $8,000 to $10,000 each—depending on the number ordered—the androids can also be rented on a daily basis. They are mounted on a self-contained unit called the Robot Cart, which contains batteries, four wheels for travel, radio controls, and tape decks. The androids can move as fast as three miles per hour on the carts. With the radio control, tape deck and voice transmitter, the androids can easily move through a crowd and sing, dance, ask and answer questions, point out merchandise—and generally mystify the crowds.

Beley feels that show or entertainment robots may be the bridge to future, more sophisticated robots because they interest businessmen like himself in utilizing them on a business, profit-making basis.

Two other entertainment robots that are quite well-known in the United States are Orion, designed by Digi-Tech, Incorporated, and Reggie the Robot, invented and designed by Ken Davis. These entertainment robots are not android in form, but look more the way we expect robots to look. Both of these robots are radio-controlled, with an operator nearby. They can sing, dance, flash lights, sell, demonstrate, and ask and answer questions. Reggie can also make weird noises, and its interior workings are visible. Orion can be dressed in different ways, according to whatever product or service it is going to sell.

Orion is dressed for a patriotic event.

Reggie the Robot with its American flag raised is ready to entertain.

Quasar Industry's sale promotional robot, Klatu, is sometimes called an entertainment robot and sometimes a home robot. Klatu comes in five different models, and Quasar Industries has announced that it will soon be selling a descendant of Klatu, their Domestic Android, for around $4,000 a unit. If it can indeed do all it promises, that will be cheap. For the Domestic Android is said to be capable of doing housework, acting as a security guard, answering the door, speaking, even educating the family! This would all be accomplished through the Domestic Android's computer and the programming unit that goes with it.

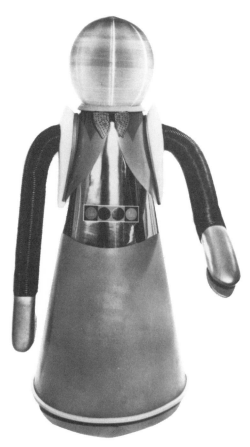

Klatu, a sales promotional robot developed by Quasar Industries.

7 Robots of the Future

The play *R.U.R.* and other plays and movies that followed were based on the idea that robots would replace humans in the labor market. Then humanity would be freed from the drudgery of work and able to enjoy life to the fullest extent. But as we saw, at least in fiction, most people are a little afraid of the idea of robot factories. Today, however, we are coming very close to having the scientific and technological know-how to produce working robots. There are already many places in the world where assembly lines are entirely automated and human beings are really not necessary for the manufacture of goods. Oil refineries, for instance, need few people to operate them. And, as in fiction, many people are feeling uncomfortable about the idea.

Some people feel that the question of robot factories is not *whether* we will have them, but *how soon*. Some are predicting that in the next ten years industrial robots will be improved to the point of being able to operate whole factories by themselves. But Joseph Engelberger, pioneer in robotics and president of Unimation, Incorporated, has said robots still have several problems to be solved: (1) improved "vision," (2) a better sense of feeling, (3) better computer interpretation of robot seeing and feeling, (4) more arms, (5) increased movement, (6) development of general-purpose robot hands, and (7) better response to voice command. Once these problems are solved, Engelberger believes the robot factory will be easily operated with few, if any, humans. In fact, an unmanned metal-working plant in Japan is already being planned.

So, in the not-too-distant future, it should be possible to manufacture goods, from the production of raw materials to the delivery and packaging of a finished product, without help of human beings. Many people are not happy about this possibility. Whenever industrial robots have been introduced, many workers and their labor unions have protested. Industries have had to compromise with the workers over their use. Sometimes the owners have had to guarantee that no workers would lose their jobs. Often industrial robots have been restricted to boring or dangerous work that no human being wants to do.

What, then, if whole factories are taken over by robots? No one really knows how workers and society may act. People must have jobs to earn money to buy the things they need. The social problems caused by robot-run industries or even the increasing use of robots have yet to be solved.

As the whole field of robotics improves, and robots become more capable and less expensive, the household robot may become common. In fact, homes may have more than one robot, each one specializing in different tasks. One robot may be for household work and one for outdoor jobs that need more strength. There may be robots specializing in care of young young children, while others may take care of the needs of those who are sick and unable to care for themselves. In fact, robots are being used right now in hospitals to train doctors and nurses. For example, one hospital robot is being used to train doctors to administer anesthesia. The robot can cough, choke, vomit, change its breathing rate, and even die!

Whether these future robots look like Andrea Android or C3PO, or are like computerized check-out registers in some grocery stores today, it seems that robots are here to stay. The growth in the use and number of modern-day robots has been closely tied to the increasing use and availability of computers and micro-processors. For, without the computer, modern robots would not be possible. The advancement of the robot is probably dependent, therefore, on the advancement of the computer.

In universities, government research centers, and private industry, considerable research is being carried out on creating artificial intelligence: computer thinking and reasoning. Although the new electronic toys seem intelligent, they are not. These toys are programmed to react to their input only in a certain way. Even those sophisticated chess-playing robots are not capable of thinking. But the future may bring a robot with artificial intelligence.

Computers can already do wonderful things. Without them, our lives today would be not much changed from the way we lived in the nineteen twenties and thirties. Computers can solve problems in millionths of a second that used to take us years to do. They can even see and talk in limited ways. As computers become increasingly more efficient in storing and processing information, they may sometime be taught how to solve problems as humans do. It is predicted that within five years a computer small enough to sit on a desk will be available with the same information storage capacity as the human brain.

With the creation of artificial intelligence and our increasing robot technology, the robots we have seen in the movies and television and read about in science fiction stories may become a reality. These robots may be able to walk, talk, and do complicated jobs, and without instructions from us, other than telling them to start. They will be able to reason—and maybe even argue—with their human owners. They will free us from the drudgery of work, save our lives, and, hopefully, help us to a better life than we have ever known. Whether this will happen in your lifetime is hard to say. Educated guesses say yes.

Index

Acupuncture, 18
Amazing Micro-Mouse
    Contest, 61
Android, 12, 13, 49, 59, 60,
    67, 70
  Andrea, 67, 76
  Adam, 67
  Domestic Android, 72, 73
Android Amusement, 67
Aquinas, Saint Thomas,
    18-19
Archytas of Tarentum, 18
Asimov, Isaac, 13
Audio-animatronics, 50
Automaton, 12, 13, 15, 16,
    17, 18, 19, 20, 21, 23,
    24, 26, 28, 32, 34, 37,
    59

Bacchus (god), 16
Battlestar Gallactica (TV
    show), 12, 48
Beley, Gene, 67, 70
Black Hole, The (movie), 48

Capek, Karel, 12
Chess Player. *See* Maelzel's
    Chess Player
Computers, 37, 38, 40, 50,
    60, 61, 62, 64, 66, 67,
    73, 76, 77

Cuckoo clocks, 21

Da Vinci, Leonardo, 19
Davis, Ken, 70
De Vaucanson, Jacques, 21,
    23, 37
  mechanical duck of, 21-23
*Day The Earth Stood Still,
    The* (movie), 48
Digi-Tech, Inc., 70
Disneyland, robots in, 50
Disneyworld, robots in, 50

Edison, Thomas, 31
Egyptian water clocks, 15
Empire Strikes Back, The
    (movie), 48
Enchanted Tiki Room, 50
Engelberger, Joseph, 75

Flight simulator, 54-55
Forbidden Planet (movie),
    48

Gallaher, John, 66
General Electric Carousel of
    Progress, 50

Hercules, hydraulically
    powered statue of, 15

Hero of Alexander, 15, 16, 17, 18, 37
Humanoid, 12, 13, 49, 51

Industrial Revolution, 23
I, Robot (book), 13

Jacquard, J.M., 23
Jaquet-Droz, Pierre, 24

Kempelen, Baron Wolfgang Von, 26, 28
Knaus, Frederick Von, 24

Lang, Fritz, 12
Link Trainer, 54
Lost in Space (TV show), 48
Lour Control Group, 64

Maelzel's Chess Player, 26, 28, 36
Magnus, Albertus, 18
Mailmobile, 46-47
Malkelyne, J.N., 31
Mars, robots on, 52
Mechanical writers, 24
Metropolis (movie), 12
Micro-processor. *See* computer

Napoleon I, 28
Nike (goddess), 17
Nuclear weapons, 56

Phantom Empire, The (movie), 48
Poe, Edgar Allen, 28

Quasar Industry, 72

Robot
   apprentices, 40, 42
   computer-controlled, 40
   crime-fighter, 56
   defined, 12
   devices, 11, 15, 32, 34, 37
   entertainment, 11, 24, 58, 67, 70, 72
   industrial, 11, 37-44, 47, 75
   kits, 58, 62, 64, 66
   mouse, 61, 62
   office, 46-47
   security, 57
   soldiers, 37, 56, 57
   toys, 58, 59, 60
   traffic, 43, 47
   weapons, 55
   Buster, 61
   Ceylon, 48
   C3PO, 48, 49, 60, 76
   Electro, 32
   et-2, 64-5
   Gort, 48
   Grivet series, 66-7
   HAL, 50
   Herman, 44-46
   Klatu, 72
   Lincoln, Abraham, 51
   Maria, 48
   Maximilian, 48
   Mike, 60
   Orion, 70
   Psycho, 31
   Ralph Roger, 67
   Reggie, 70

Robby, 48, 50
R2D2, 48, 49, 59, 67
Six, 67
Sparko, 33
Turtle, 62-64
V.I.N.CENT, 48
"Robota," 12
Robotics, Asimov's three
  laws of, 13-14
R.U.R. (Rossum's Universal
  Robots), 12, 74

Seismometer, 53
Sensors, 47, 57, 63, 64
Sleeper (movie), 48
Space Shuttle, 54
Star Trek (TV show and
  movie), 48
Star Wars (movie), 12, 48,
  49, 67
Strasbourg Cathedral clock,
  20
Striking-jacks, 19

Terrapin, Inc., 62
Thermostat, 13
Three Mile Island Nuclear
  Power Plant, 44
Tobar the Great (movie), 48

Unimation, 75
United States, robots in, 58,
  70
U.S. Department of Energy,
  44

Viking landers, 52-53

"Wall huggers." *See* robot
  mouse
War of the Worlds (movie),
  48
World's Fair, in New York
  City, 32, 33
World War II, 34, 54